Steps to Greatness

Caroline Katko

Steps to Greatness © 2021

Caroline Katko

Presentation by *BookLeaf Publishing*

Web: www.bookleafpub.com

E-mail: info@bookleafpub.com

ISBN: 978-93-5744-869-7

First edition 2021

To my eighth grade English teacher, Mrs. Newman. Thank you for introducing me to the wonderful world of poetry!

ACKNOWLEDGEMENT

First off, thanks to all of the wonderful people at BookLeaf Publishing. I never in a million years thought I would have the opportunity to publish a book. Thank you for taking a chance on a new writer.

Next, I would like to thank my mom for her endless support of my journey through writing and life.

Finally, I would like to thank my friends for giving me input in the early stages of writing and for encouraging me in times of doubt.

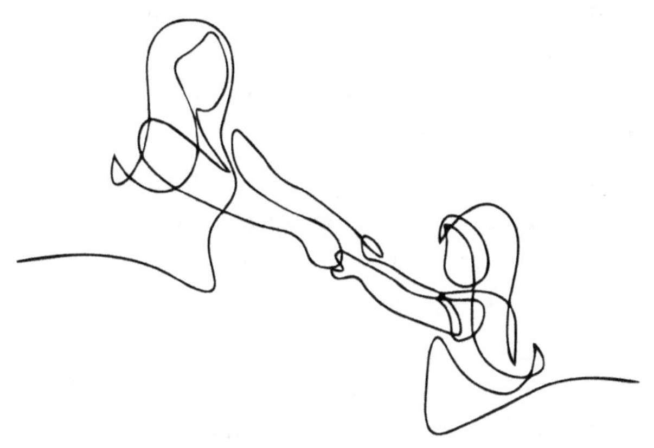

first poem

As I gape over the wide ocean
Realising I told myself, a hundred lies
I feel the depth of the emotion
I once noticed in your gleaming eyes
When your wet lips were trying in vain
To reveal something, I surmise
Yet you could not reap any gain
For I was the unfortunate, the unwise
Who couldn't understand your helpless voice,
Your silent, motionless gesture
I took no pain, I left you no choice
Now you're gone forever.

I can't yet but curse my fate
The time is gone when I could have chosen you
My mate
You expressed love, only I understood it too late

first love

You entered and you passed by—
Cupid whispered to me
through the passing wind
And the deafening storm
the harbingers, your footsteps formed.
You passed by me, towering tall
I stood still, a petrified call.
You looked my way
and flashed a smile
The elixir pouring from your eyes
soothing, calming the leper bound
Deep within my heart's lies.

touch me not

Touch me not! a plant being yells
It's scared someone will heighten the hell's
agony it is trying to suppress

Legend of yore, if I recall
says a girl fell in love with a lad tall
She was an oyster with a hidden pearl
a beauty, a soft hearted girl
The boy was a magnificent prince
a fierce shark with large fins

Together they loved, so they lived.

The boy touched her heart, she giggled with
mirth

Not for long, he was a cheat
He left her astound

She closed her heart long ago
But still she does cry when any human
beast's shadow passes by

"Closed have I, my heart from you, it will
be protected from thou,

Love forgotten, infatuation sought,
But please
Touch me not!"

science exhibition

We never reached the high school building.
Because there was a corridor leading to high
school,
And there was a collapsible gate at the corridor
corner
And when we were passing the gate
I saw sunshine outside
like marshmallow melting through rain
I had never peeped inside the gate, it was
forbidden
I was holding her hand, so it was easy
to pull her and enter the gate
Inside was a courtyard of abandoned flowers
Zinnias, gerberas, and petunias
It was a small patch, a corner some sister
Would have claimed as her own
Like Mendel, to grow her own children
I took my sweet, lowly flower into the patch
We cut the small path
and smelled the nectar in the rain
I found the smallest nook under the eaves,
Where only the flowers could see us
And tasted the nectar of her lips
Over and over.
She groped my neck, I bit her petals,

I inhaled her musk, from her sweater,
I heard her moan, and sucked her tongue,
and kissed her till the end of dawn.

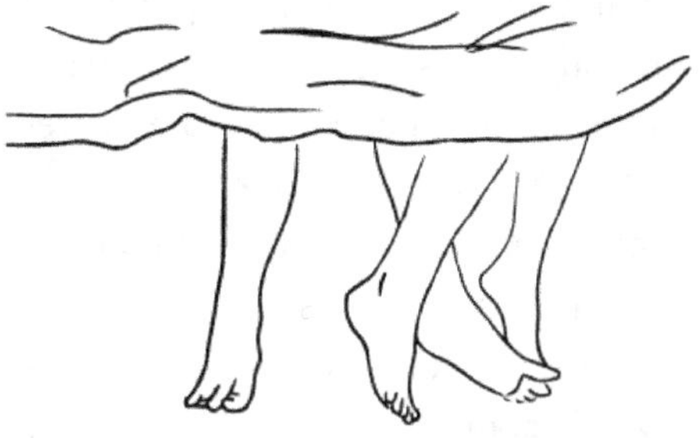

first depression

Love is like an oasis in a hot desert
Giving a ray of hope among the hurt
Sometimes it's like the first shower of rain
In the springtime, cooling the depressed brain
Love is not so easy a matter
Innumerable hearts it can shatter
Loved ones nor love is a possession
True love is actually never an obsession
Love is about always giving, not getting
It's like a universal play that's got no ending.

corny poem

Your appealing smile drives me crazy
how can I ever describe the depth to you daisy

Of the ocean of my love, my commitment
for I well know you and I can never be in a tent

Where no one shall stir our intense love
and we can live happily like two dove

You and I can never be one
it has been sworn by the sun

For we are not made for each other
and still there exists someone for both of us
farther

Nevertheless, I shall never forget your presence
it shall remain in my heart as dense

As it was always. I shall never abandon
my faith in you and thy lord's pardon

I believe, I trust, I shall continue to trust
till I die, that we shall meet

We shall be reunited in love's heat
whatever be we in this life's entanglement
somewhere, sometime we shall be the same segment
drown in deep, intense, love, love, love.

hope

Casted in the mirror was a shade,
Soon, it seemed to fade
How to restore the peace of mind
Caused by — the shade behind
Held a shine in the eyes, quite mundane
Sparkling, gleaming with earthly pain
The gait was taciturn
Revealing an infinitely tormenting burn

A phoenix rising from the ash mansion
In search of lost love, lost passion.

fear of abandonment

Can you hear my voice there?
Miles and miles away from me, far away
The melancholy it sings, loud sway
Can you feel my heart wear?

Can you see my image there?
Searching for you, where you have lost
The desperate sight, the impenetrable frost
Can you feel my eyes tear?

Can you feel my love there, now that I'm not
here?
Needing your care, your smile to heal the sore
Can you feel the seeds of love growing
even in the loneliest of tombs,
Can you see the new life being born
even in the darkest of the wombs?

always hopeful

A day before yester, a jester before today
My love asketh me, how, how much you love
say;
I laugh at you love for asking such a foolish
And remark it is infinite, making life hellish

Now, at present glory, when I sit alone missed
And tears stain the very face you once kissed
I asketh myself that very thought, the love once
sought.

No! My mind says to my heart, this is not love
exact.
For when the flame burns high and low, the
nature of love will be sacked,
And so I steal, upon the precious grains of time
And wander around the world in search of a
similar crime.

Lo, go, go and and go, yeah here
There is that little hungry child, filled with fear
Her tiny hands spread like a lotus leaf
And my heart says, "Yeah this is my love—
poor, yet not a thief."

Lo, go, go and and go, yeah here
There in the flowery meadow, stands a seer
A blind fellow, eyes blank like sky cloudless
And my heart sings, "Yeah this is my love—
blind, yet not sightless."

Lo, go, go and and go, yeah here
There in the lake near, sits an idle peer
eyes filled with dreams, shattered and tattered,
He slings a few pebbled on the surface
smothered

And now my heart moans,
"Sure this is my love not— perhaps painful and
dreamless, yet filled with hope endless."

Hope

To all who questioned me

Or doubted me
Or convinced me I wasn't enough
Congratulations

There are many ways a person can be broken
And I have shattered into a thousand pieces

However
If a broken heart can learn to love again
And if a broken leg can run again
Then a broken soul can learn to feel again
Hope is precious
Never let it go

Doubt

Even though the light is bright
I can't escape with all my might
No matter how hard I fight

Because the source of my pain
Is locked in my brain
And I writhe in vain

They say that suffering makes you stronger
But I don't know how I can make it any longer
Even though it feels so much more wrong

I stiffen and brace
As the tears flow down my face
Like an endless race

Is it a crime
To fear I'm out of time
And past my prime
It's time to draw the line
And no, I'm not fine
I'm just strangled by a vine

It's very rough
And I'm not that tough
And I'll never be enough

Everyday I quake
Waiting for my big break
And I must pretend I'm fake

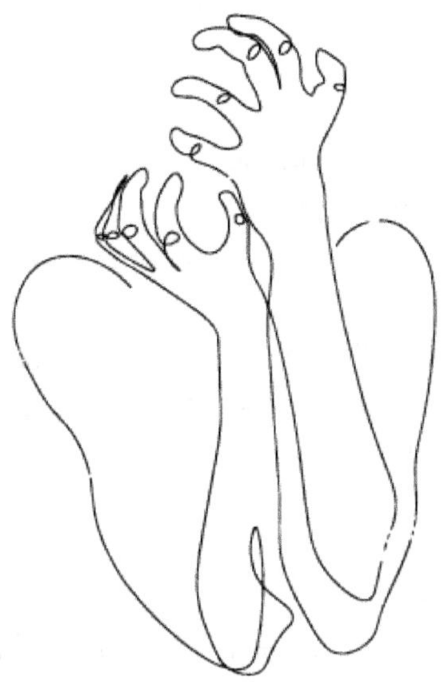

Ambitions

Joy rises in your stomach
Your heart beats fast
The table rocks from the tapping of an anxious
hand
It's been a while since you've truly felt this way
You almost can't believe it
But it's real
Excitement
Anticipation
Confidence
It's been a while since your last big win
And once again
You're looking towards the future
To see how it all unfolds

Hard Work

They say everything happens for a reason
But I'm not sure
Some were born to suffer
But others were born to thrive
Can great things come to those who suffer?
Can pain come to those who rise?
Yes
The risers have heavy chains on their ankles
But the sinkers have wings
If they can't break free, the risers fall
Those who fall are trapped until they discover
their wings
But it's not that simple
Your wings can be clipped at any moment
And may take time to heal
Shackles can break at any time
Anyone can rise or fall
But those who fight the chains from early on
Develop stronger wings because they didn't stop
pulling
All the strain and all of the struggle built up the
wings
So the second the chains break, they can go
higher and faster
Than those who never strained
And those who never took the time

To grow their wings

Strength

You break a bone
It grows back stronger
Taking more force to break again
As it continues to strengthen
Blow after blow
The power continues to grow
Until the force cannot break it
The bone that has been broken time and again
Is now stronger than the rest
And when a single blow
Ripples through the whole body
The bone that was beaten
Bruised
Broken
Is the bone that survives
And you are the bone that is still standing
Even when the rest cannot

Courage

Wisdom without ambition
Is like a sea with no boats
Its vastness stretches endless
But will never be discovered
Use your inner drive
Go out and explore that vast ocean
Paddle beyond the horizon
Into the uncertainty
Yes, you may discover something bad
But what about the chance of discovering
something good?
The unknown holds many mysteries
And can be frightening
Because chances are
It's unlike anything you've ever seen before

Scars

Do you know what it feels like to have your own
mind betray you?
Swimming in darkness with no way out?
You are blind, clawing desperately for an escape
Little do you know, people are trying to help, but
you just can't see them
All you can see are the people who are numb to
your scratches
Gasping for air you claw the few who hear your
screams
And don't even realize it
As blood drips down their hand, you continue to
blindly claw
They don't give up
You rip them to shreds in panic
But they stay
Some people leave, your scratches were too
much for them
But some still stay
You slowly crawl into the light
You look at the blood under your nails and
wonder
What have I done?
You rub your eyes gently as they adjust to the
light
There are footprints from those who left

But red puddles on the ground from those who
stayed
It's a long, brutal process as you pick up the mop
When your hands start to shake, you squeeze the
wood harder
Slowly, the blood dries up, and you can wipe it
away
But little do you know, that was the easy part
You find the people you've hurt, curled up and
bleeding on the floor
You grab their wounded hands and wipe
You wipe the blood away and begin to stitch
Now you wait for the healing
Some didn't have the patience for healing
So they walked away
But the even smaller number that remained heal
quickly
Now you are left to clean yourself up
You scrub your nails clean and wash your hands
As you wash, you take the time to notice your
own scars
Scars from when you tried to help others
And refused to leave them
Most people left you open and bleeding
But few helped to repair the damage they've
caused
I don't want to be like them
Like those who left
That's why I take my time

To wipe the blood from the floor

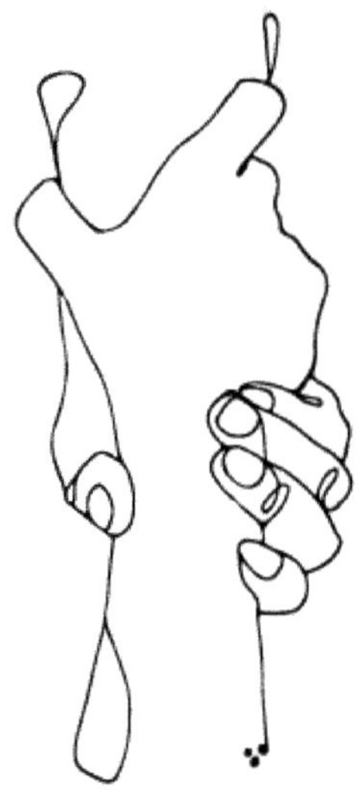

Soldiers

It hurts so bad
Your world is falling apart
And all you can do is stand there
Chained to the wall
And as the wall begins to fall
And it feels there's nothing left
Nothing left to feel
So you don't feel
Just close your eyes and go numb
Your screams ripple through your world
All around the room
Over and under
Some hear but choose to ignore
Others don't even notice
But all it takes
Is for one person
To return the scream
To know
You're not alone
Not the only one screaming
As you push blindly through the dark room
And find each other
Only then can the pain unclench
Only then can you find silence
Only then can you find peace

Passion

Word by word
Page by page
Flipping through the pages of life
Waiting for an engaging chapter
That never comes
And it never will
Until you write it
Don't just write anything
Write from your head
Heart
And everything in between
By digging word for word
You touch your inner soul
It reminds you
Don't write just anything
Write something worth writing
Write something worthy of you

Pain

The familiar burning rises from the pit of your
stomach
Up your back
Into your head
Your pulse dances wildly in your limbs
A warm teardrop rolls down your face
And onto your lips with its salty taste
Your eyes blur as you feel yourself sinking
Sinking so far down
That you don't know if you'll ever be pulled out
A warm blade is plunged into your stomach
And twists slowly with every tear that falls
With all your remaining strength
You reach upward
All you see is people above
Reaching
But they are too far
And all they can do
Is watch you sink into the darkness

Memories

Many are haunted by their past
The hardships
Struggles
Trauma
And fear
The past is like a weight
Strapped to your ankle
In the middle of the ocean
You can see the surface
But can't quite break through
You strain and struggle against the mighty
weight
Desperate for an escape
But there is only one way out
The weight will always be there
It is a part of who you are
The only way to break the surface
Is to swim down to the ocean floor
Through the cavern of memories
Some are beautiful
Some are haunting
But you cannot stop swimming
Or you will be trapped
You must reach the bottom and claw the weight
Claw through the pain
Terror

And heartbreak
You sigh at the lighter weight
Swimming through the surface
Where you can see the sun

Power

Thoughts are like the ocean
The tide comes in
Leaving you trapped under water
And goes out
Leaving you parched
The cycle repeats
In
And out
In
And out
And when the water is still
Calm enough to see your reflection
The curve of your face
The reflection in your eye
You see your polished face
Smoothed by the rocking of the tide
Your skin is smooth and fair
And your mind is
Calm
Your golden eyes open and see
There is a whole world out here
And I finally get to see it

Persistence

The mountain peak stands so high
And I wonder if I can get by
All I want is to touch the sky
And scream
I made it
Because I faked it
Until I did it
And now you all get to witness
My persistence
Through the resistance
And my insistence
With little assistance
And those who failed me?
Good riddance
They made little difference
In my struggle of perseverance

Confidence

You know that you can do it
You know you can achieve it
But you worry what others will think
The line between confidence and arrogance is
blurry
But also very clear
Arrogance is knowing that you're great
While confidence is believing you could be
Many who cross that line will fall
But those who stand at the line
And look into the horizon
And think
'I see the greatness'
'Now I just need to be the greatness'

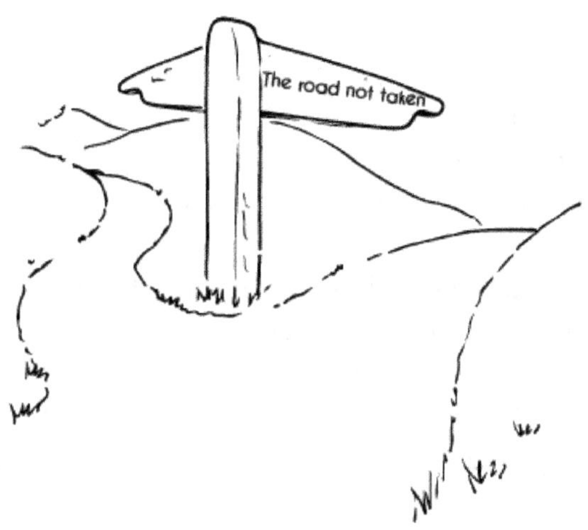
The road not taken

Struggle

Everyday I try my best
But it's never enough to impress
It's like my struggle is expected
But never praised
It's like the world looks at me and decides
"She's not in enough pain
Let's double it and smile"
And if I overcome it
They laugh and say
"Game on
You don't even know what it means
To suffer
Let's turn off the lights
Shackle her ankles
And stab from all directions
Nevermind
Leave the lights on
And put a mirror
We want her to witness her own downfall"

Weapons

How can something be so good
So powerful yet twisted
So beautiful but painful
Fulfilling and crippling
How can something so special and wonderful
Cause so much pain and suffering
Like black and white
A double-edged blade
That carves a path
While ripping into skin
The blade that is coated with glory
Is also wet with blood
The blood that no one else can see
And only I can feel

Determination

They send you on a journey
That few can complete
You climb the mountain `
They say you were too slow
You cross the desert
But given no water
Walk through a forest
While blindfolded
Swim through the river
In the dead of winter
Defeat a demon
With no weapon
And when you're through
Having given it your all
And collapsing at their feet
Starved
Cold
Bruised
Bleeding
They say
You were never good enough

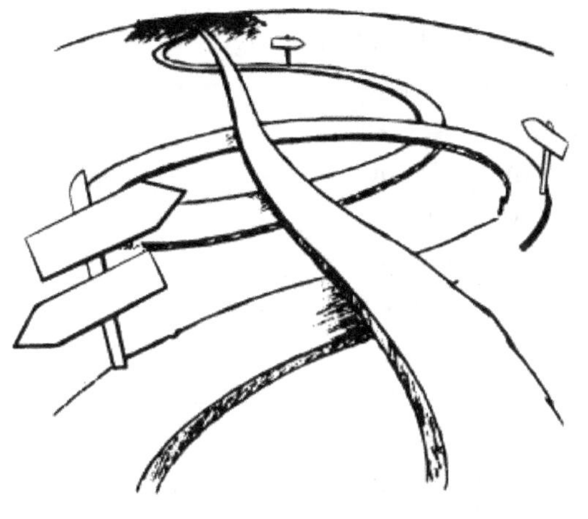

Balance

You can never do anything right
It's not good enough
Work harder
Is what they tell you
You try to ignore it
To just push through
But that is your biggest mistake
Let it in
Let the pressure grow
But only on your terms
Because the right pressure can make a diamond
But the wrong pressure can make dust
In a room full of dust
Be a diamond

Bold

Some call it different
Some odd
Some strange
Because the one who was always different
Left the dark shadow they were stuck in
And flinched as the spotlight hit their face
Their eyelids flutter
And their pupils shrink
But they still look up
As their sharp edges show
But they don't push back
They push forward
Feeling all eyes on their flaws
But their eyes stay up
As the crowd stays down
As they walk back into the shadows
Leaving people hypnotized

Devotion

To those who came before me
Who I am made from
I would like to welcome you to a fascinating
place
One you created
But never got to see
Welcome to my mind
You may find yourself peering into a woven
mirror
That has slightly distorted over time
This place is of complex origin
Strange
Unique
Truth-seeking
With its sights set on changing the world
After all
An Empire starts with a single mind
A mind who had the encouragement to do so
A mind who saw the future
And what it could become

Greatness

What is greatness?
What does it take to be great?
Is it boldness?
Was it written in my fate?
I must have awareness
Did I start my path too late?
I struggle with my indecisiveness
Who cares, I'll never wait
I'm too full of wishfulness
I have much at stake
How much of me is fake?
I must bend but never break
None, I practice kindness
And do whatever it will take
But others say it's blindness
Against a world full of hate
I need more willfulness
Where many will underestimate
To overcome this viciousness
My ability to create
Even when in sickness
Even when my hands vibrate
I must hold persistence
Doesn't mean I can't operate
In a world of passiveness
I just need time to regulate

I must maintain my hopefulness
Now I can be the ultimate
That I will achieve greatness
I guess that's what makes me great

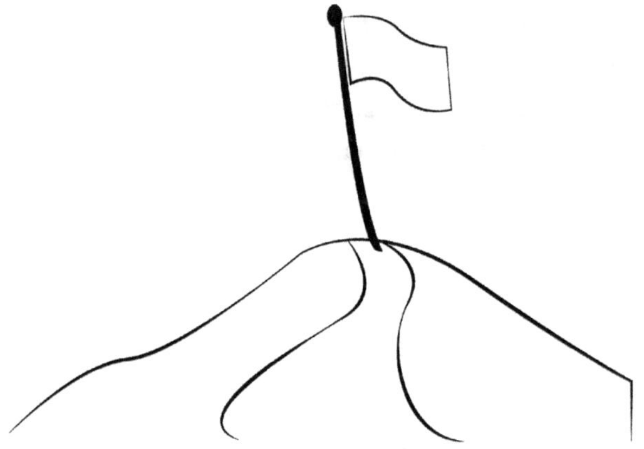